Made in the USA
Monee, IL
11 October 2021

79802520R00056